JN089194

CNN Short News for Listening Business

JACET Material Design & Development SIG

Asahi Press

音声再生アプリ「リスニング・トレーナー」を使った音声ダウンロード

朝日出版社開発のアプリ、「リスニング・トレーナー（リストレ）」を使えば、教科書の音声を
スマホ、タブレットに簡単にダウンロードできます。どうぞご活用ください。

◉ アプリ【リスニング・トレーナー】の使い方

《アプリのダウンロード》

App Store または Google Play から
「リスニング・トレーナー」のアプリ
（無料）をダウンロード

App Storeは
こちら▶

Google Playは
こちら▶

《アプリの使い方》

① アプリを開き「コンテンツを追加」をタップ
② 画面上部に【15718】を入力しDoneをタップ

音声・映像ストリーミング配信 》》

この教科書の音声及び、
付属の映像は、
右記ウェブサイトにて
無料で配信しています。

https://text.asahipress.com/free/english/

はじめに

　本書は、ビジネスをテーマとした短い英語ニュースを、世界最大のニュース専門メディアCNN放送から15本選りすぐって収録したものです。1本のニュースは、集中力を維持しながら聞き通せる約30秒の長さで、重要な情報がコンパクトにまとめられています。

　ビジネスといっても経済・金融情報という狭義の捉え方ではなく、労働、雇用などビジネスを取り巻く社会情勢や、最新のビジネストレンドやハイテクなど我々のライフスタイルにも影響を及ぼすような幅広い話題が取り上げられています。さらに、ジェンダー、ロボット開発、宇宙開発事業など今後のビジネス機会の拡大を予測させる話題にも触れています。ビジネスの最前線で活躍している企業家の活動やトップ企業の経営戦略や動向などを知ることにより、アメリカを中心に世界で実際に何が起こっているのか、何が問題になっているのかなどに関して見聞を広め、時事問題に対する思考の糧を得られます。

　ニュース音声は、CNNの放送そのものである「ナチュラル音声」のほか、ナレーターがゆっくり音読した「ポーズ（無音の間）入り」と「ポーズなし」の音声が用意されています。このような3パターンの音声を［30秒×3回聞き］方式に従ってリスニング練習を行うと、最初はアンカーが話す速度が速すぎて聞き取れないと思われるニュース英語でも聞き取れるようになれます。さらに、通訳者養成学校でも採用されているサイトトランスレーション（速訳）や区切り聞き、シャドーイングといった学習法と組みあわせて練習することにより効果的にリスニング力を向上させることができます。詳細は、巻頭の「3つの効果的な学習法+α」に説明されていますので、実際の練習前に目を通しておくことをお勧めします。

　ニュースのリスニングにはいわゆる5W1H（Who, What, When, Where, Why, How）の情報を理解することが重要です。TOEIC-Style Questions などで内容に関する理解を深めた後、ニュースの持つ意味合い（implications）を考え、提起された問題などを英語もしくは日本語で語り合ってください。本書で学習することにより、リスニングを中心とした英語の総合力を身に付け、さらに時事問題にも関心を高められますことを切望しております。

　最後になりましたが、本書の執筆にあたり、編集部の加藤愛理氏をはじめ、朝日出版社のスタッフの方々には多大なるご支援、ご協力を戴きました。心より感謝申し上げます。

2023年10月
著者一同

CONTENTS

目次

本書の使い方

1ページ目で、英語のみでキーワードとキーフレーズを利用してニュースの内容を理解してみましょう。2ページ目で、日本語の語注とトランスクリプトを利用して、ニュースの内容を理解してみましょう。3ページ目で、「3つの効果的な学習法＋α」を利用して学習しましょう。4ページ目で、ニュースの話題に関連した背景知識や語句を学習することにより学習を発展させましょう。

(1ページ目)

● Listen and check the words ❶

2回ナチュラル音声を聞いて、ニュースの内容理解に必要なキーワードとなる5つの単語を聞き取れた時に、□にチェックを入れてみてください。そして、それぞれの単語の定義を参考にしながら、英語のみで内容を理解してみましょう。

● Listen and check the words ❷

2回ポーズが入っていないゆっくり音声を聞いて、ニュースの内容理解に必要なキーフレーズ（語句）を聞き取れた時に、□にチェックを入れてみてください。そして、それぞれのキーフレーズの前後に聞き取れた語句を加えて、さらに内容理解を深めましょう。

● Check your comprehension

キーワードやキーフレーズならびにその前後のフレーズを聞き取った後、ニュースの内容を書いてみましょう。内容理解を深めた後、ニュースのタイトルにふさわしいものを選んでみましょう。

(2ページ目)

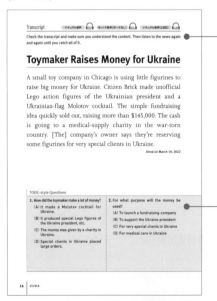

● Transcript

トランスクリプトを見ながら、ナチュラル音声やゆっくり音声を聞いて、1ページ目で理解した内容と合っているか確かめてみてください。そして、さらにニュースの内容理解を深めてみましょう。

● TOEIC-style Questions

ニュースの内容理解を確認するために、TOEIC形式の問題に挑戦してみましょう。

●Transcript divided by slashes

「3つの効果的な学習法＋α」にある①速読能力が高まるサイトトランスレーション、②速聴能力が高まる区切り聞き、③総合力を養うシャドーイング、④主述の一致の英語学習法を利用してみましょう。

●ニュースのミニ知識

ニュースで取り上げられている内容をさらに理解できるように情報を加えています。

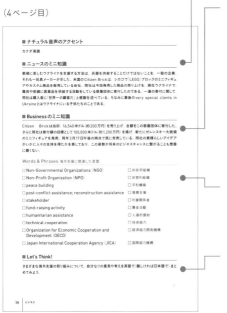

●Business のミニ知識

ニュースに登場する企業やその企業のトップリーダーの動向についての情報を中心に、ニュース関連のビジネスのトピックに特化した背景知識を身につけるための短い読み物です。背景知識をつけることにより、情報を深く分析でき、さらにトピックに対する問題意識を高めることができます。情勢は刻一刻と変化していきますが、ニュースの背景を知っていると最新の関連ニュースを聞いたり、読んだりするときにも一段と理解が深まります。

●Words & Phrases

ニュースには使用されていませんが、ニュースの話題に関連した重要語句を記載しています。同じトピックで類似のニュースを聞いたり、読んだりするときにも理解の足掛かりとなる重要な情報です。

●Let's Think!

ニュースのトピックに対する問題意識を持ち、発展学習としてリサーチしたり、自分なりの意見や考えを英語あるいは日本語でまとめましょう。discussion のテーマとしても最適です。

3つの効果的な学習法＋α

　本書は「30秒×3回聞き」方式を採用しています。これによって、だれでも世界標準の英語ニュースが聞き取れるようになるはずです。

　「30秒×3回聞き」方式とは、30秒という集中力が途切れない長さのニュースを、3種類の音声で聞くというものです。そのため、ご提供する音声（音声の入手・再生方法については p.2 を参照）は、各ニュースが「ナチュラル音声」、「ゆっくり音声（ポーズ入り）」、「ゆっくり音声（ポーズなし）」という3種類で収録されています。また、文字としてもそれらに対応する形の英文が掲載されています。

　これらの音声や英文は、ただ単に聞いたり読んだりするのではなく、以下に示すサイトトランスレーション、区切り聞き、シャドーイングという3つの学習法と結びつけることで高い効果を生むようになっています。

❶速読能力が高まるサイトトランスレーション

　俗に「サイトラ」と呼ばれます。英語でつづると sight translation です。sight は、名詞として「視力、視覚」、形容詞として「見てすぐの、初見での」という意味を持ちます。目にしたところからすぐに訳していくのが sight translation です。

　サイトラの練習では、英文を頭から語順通りに目で追い、情報・意味の区切り目と思われる個所にスラッシュ（／）を書き入れ、区切られた部分をすぐに訳します。それを英文の最後まで次々と繰り返すのですが、こうした訳し方を「順送りの訳」と呼ぶこともあります。

　なお、英文をどのくらい細かく区切るか、どこを情報・意味の区切り目としてスラッシュを入れるかは人それぞれでよく、絶対的なルールがあるわけではありません。

（利点・効能）サイトラを行うと、書かれた英文がその語順通りに理解できるようになり、自然と「速読」に結びつきます。そして、英文を素早く理解できるようになるということは、英文を英文としてそのまま理解できるということにつながっていきます。また、「読んで分からないものは聞いても分からない」という原則に従えば、サイトラの速読能力が「区切り聞き」で養う速聴能力の土台になるといえます。

（本書での学習法）本書では、各ニュースの放送音声を文字に書き起こし、普通の英文

（transcript）とスラッシュで区切られた英文（transcript divided by slashes）の形で掲載しています。まずはスラッシュで区切られた英文を順番にどんどん訳していく練習をしましょう。

　本書で示されたスラッシュの入れ方はあくまで一例です。これに従ってしばらく練習しているとサイトラのやり方が感覚的につかめてきますので、やり方が分かったら、普通の英文を自分なりの区切り方で訳してみると、よい練習になります。

練習のポイント サイトラはなるべく素早く行うことが大切です。英文は「読んだ端から消えていくもの」くらいに考えて、次々と順送りの訳をこなしていきましょう。そうしているうちに読むスピードが速くなるはずですし、区切り聞きにもつながります。

❷速聴能力が高まる区切り聞き

　サイトラをリスニングのトレーニングに応用したのが、「区切り聞き」と呼ばれる学習法です。サイトラでは英語が目から入ってきましたが、区切り聞きでは英語が耳から入ってくることになります。

　区切り聞きの場合、英文にスラッシュを入れる代わりに、情報・意味の区切り目と思われる個所でオーディオプレーヤーを一時停止させ、すぐに訳します。その部分を訳し終えたら再び音声を先に進め、同様の作業を繰り返していきます。

利点・効能 区切り聞きを行うと、話された英文がその語順通りに理解できるようになり、自然と「速聴」に結びつきます。そして、英文を素早く理解できるようになるということは、英文を英文としてそのまま理解できるということにつながっていきます。

本書での学習法 だれでも英語ニュースが聞き取れるようになるよう、本書では区切り聞き練習を重視しています。ご提供する音声に収録されている「ゆっくり音声（ポーズ入り）」を利用することで、オーディオプレーヤーを自分でいちいち一時停止させる面倒がなくなり、区切り聞きがしやすくなっています。ポーズ（無音の間）の位置はサイトラのスラッシュと同じにしてありますが、ポーズで区切られた部分を素早く訳していきましょう。

音声には、各ニュースが「ナチュラル音声」、「ゆっくり音声（ポーズ入り）」、「ゆっくり音声（ポーズなし）」の順番で入っています。まずは「ナチュラル音声」を聞いて全体の内容を推測し、次に「ゆっくり音声（ポーズ入り）」を使った区切り聞きで部分ごとに順番に理解できるようになり、その後「ゆっくり音声（ポーズなし）」で全体を頭から素早く理解していくことができるかどうか試してみてください。

　なお、最後には、全ニュースのナチュラル音声だけを集めて、もう一度収録してあります。これらを頭から素早く理解していけるようになるのが最終目標です。

練習のポイント　音声は流れる端から消えていってしまいます。英文を後ろから前に戻って理解するなどということはできないため、耳に入った文を瞬時に理解する英語力と集中力が求められます。このトレーニングによってリスニング力は必ず向上するので、集中力を高める訓練をするつもりで挑戦してみましょう。

　特にニュースを聞く場合、背景知識があると情報がすんなりと頭に入りますから、日ごろからいろいろな記事について興味を持っておくことも大切です。本書には「ニュースのミニ知識」が掲載されているので、役立ててください。

　英文は論理的と言われますが、特にニュースでは、全体の起承転結の流れはもちろん、ひとつのセンテンスの中でも、「①だれ（何）が ②だれ（何）に対して ③何を ④いつ ⑤どこで」という情報がかなり秩序だって含まれています。このような情報を意識して聞くと、リスニングも楽になります。

❸総合力を養うシャドーイング

　シャドーイングは英語でshadowingとつづります。shadowという語には動詞として「影のように付いていく」という意味がありますが、学習法としてのシャドーイングは、聞こえてくる英語音声を一歩後から追いかけるようにリピートしていくものです。オリジナルの英語音声に遅れないように付いていく様子が「影」のようなので、こう名づけられました。

利点・効能　シャドーイングは、今聞いた音声をリピートしながら、同時に次の音声のリスニングも行うというものなので、アウトプットとインプットの同時進行になります。その

ため同時通訳のトレーニングとして普及しましたが、一般の英語学習者にも有益であることがいろいろな研究で認められています。

通常のリスニング練習は学習者が音声を聞くだけ、すなわち受動的なやり方であるのに対し、シャドーイングは学習者の参加を伴うもの、いわば能動的な学習法です。この能動的な学習法は、受動的なものに比べ、よりいっそう集中力を高める訓練になり、リスニング力を向上させます。また、正しい発音やイントネーションを身につける訓練にもなり、ひいてはスピーキング力を高めるのにも役立ちます。

本書での学習法 シャドーイングは難易度の高い学習法なので、「ナチュラル音声」でいきなり練習するのではなく、最初は「ゆっくり音声（ポーズなし）」を利用するのがよいでしょう。それでも難しいと感じる人も多いでしょうから、「ゆっくり音声（ポーズ入り）」から始めるのも一案です。ポーズが入った音声を用いるのは本来のシャドーイングとは違うという考え方もありますが、無理をして挫折することのないよう、まずはできることから始めてください。

練習のポイント シャドーイングでは、流れてくる音声を一字一句リピートしなければならないため、ひとつひとつの単語に神経を集中するあまり、文全体の意味を把握できなくなることがよくあります。きちんと論旨を追いながらトレーニングすることが大切です。

ただし、区切り聞きのように日本語に順次訳していこうと思ってはいけません。英語を正確に聞き取り、正確な発音とイントネーションでリピートしようとしているときに、頭の中に日本語を思い浮かべていては混乱するだけだからです。シャドーイングには、区切り聞きから一歩進んで、英語を英語のまま理解する力が必要になってきます。

もしも英語でのシャドーイングがどうしても難しすぎるという場合は、まず日本語でシャドーイングする練習から始めてみましょう。

＋α（プラスアルファ）の学習法

◆主述の一致

　主語と述語動詞を一致させる問題はTOEICでよく出題されます。主語の人称（1人称、2人称、3人称）や数（単数・複数）によって、be動詞・一般動詞の現在形やbe動詞の過去形など適切なものを選ばなければなりません。また、接続詞で結ばれた複合主語もあり、複数ある主語のうちどの主語に述語動詞を一致させるかにも注意しなければなりません。

　主語となる名詞には○印を、動詞には下線を引くなどして、主述が一致していることを確かめてみてください。

利点・効果 TOEICやTOEFL ITPなどの主述の一致問題の対策にもなります。また、主述の一致を意識することで、会話や英作文といった英語使用のアウトプットの際に役立つことにもなります。

本書での学習法 主語となる名詞と一致させる動詞を探しながら、品詞を理解することで文構造が見えてきます。速読をした後、品詞を理解しながら語注を参考にして精読にも挑戦してみましょう。さらに、各UnitにあるTOEIC形式の問題にも挑戦してみてください。

学習のポイント 文の要素として、主語となるのは複数の語で形成される主部（名詞句）や主部のなかで中心となる語（名詞）です。まずは、主部を見つけ、次に主部のなかで中心となる語（名詞）を探してみましょう。次に、述語動詞を探し、主語の人称や数と一致しているか確認してみてください。主語には、複合主語や省略もありますので注意してください。

Unit 1:「ゼレンスキーレゴ」が即完売!

🔊)) Listen and check the words ❶

ナチュラル音声 🎧 02

Listen two times to the news read at natural speed. Check the box for each of the keywords below when you hear them, and look at the definition of each word to understand the news.

definition

- ☐ raise   [reɪz]   : to collect money or people together
- ☐ unofficial   [ˌʌnəˈfɪʃəl]   : that does not have approval from somebody in authority
- ☐ fundraising   [ˈfʌndˌreɪzɪŋ]   : collecting money available for a particular purpose
- ☐ charity   [tʃærɪti]   : an organization for helping people in need
- ☐ client   [klaɪənt]   : a person who uses the services of a professional organization

🔊)) Listen and check the words ❷

ゆっくり音声[ポーズなし] 🎧 04

Listen two times to the same news read at slow speed without pauses. Check the box for each of the words or phrases below when you hear them, and write down any other information or expressions you hear.

- ☐ action figure
- ☐ Molotov cocktail
- ☐ war-torn
- ☐ medical-supply
- ☐ reserve A for B

Notes

Check your comprehension

What is the news about?

Headline

Choose the best headline for this news.

(A) Lego Action Figures for Clients in Ukraine

(B) Toymaker Raises Money for Ukraine

(C) Toymaker Invests over $145,000

(D) Unofficial Lego of Ukraine President

Check the transcript and make sure you understand the content. Then listen to the news again and again until you catch all of it.

Toymaker Raises Money for Ukraine

A small toy company in Chicago is using little figurines to raise big money for Ukraine. Citizen Brick made unofficial Lego action figures of the Ukrainian president and a Ukrainian-flag Molotov cocktail. The simple fundraising idea quickly sold out, raising more than $145,000. The cash is going to a medical-supply charity in the war-torn country. [The] company's owner says they're reserving some figurines for very special clients in Ukraine.

Aired on March 19, 2022

TOEIC-style Questions

1. How did the toymaker make a lot of money?
   (A) It made a Molotov cocktail for Ukraine.
   (B) It produced special Lego figures of the Ukraine president, etc.
   (C) The money was given by a charity in Ukraine.
   (D) Special clients in Ukraine placed large orders.

2. For what purpose will the money be used?
   (A) To launch a fundraising-company
   (B) To support the Ukraine president
   (C) For very special clients in Ukraine
   (D) For medical care in Ukraine

Use this page to practice slash listening and shadowing. Circle the subject and underline the verb to understand subject-verb agreement.

「ゼレンスキーレゴ」が即完売！

RUSSIA INVADES UKRAINE
TOY COMPANY RAISES $145K+ FOR UKRAINE WITH

A small toy company in Chicago is using little figurines /
to raise big money for Ukraine. //
Citizen Brick made unofficial Lego action figures /
of the Ukrainian president /
and a Ukrainian-flag Molotov cocktail. //
The simple fundraising idea quickly sold out, /
raising more than $145,000. //
The cash is going to a medical-supply charity /
in the war-torn country. //
[The] company's owner says /
they're reserving some figurines for very special clients in Ukraine. //

語注

toymaker: 玩具メーカー	非公式の	**fundraising:** 資金調達の、資金集めの	**charity:** 慈善団体
raise: （資金などを）調達する、集める	**Lego:** レゴ ▶デンマーク生まれのブロック玩具	**sell out:** 売り切れる、完売する	**war-torn:** 戦争で荒れた、戦禍を被った
figurine: ミニフィギュア	**action figure:** 人型模型、フィギュア	**cash:** 現金	**owner:** 経営者
Citizen Brick: シチズンブリック ▶レゴのカスタムパーツを製造・販売する会社	**president:** 大統領	**go to:** （金などが）〜に回される	**reserve A for B:** AをB のために取っておく
unofficial:	**Ukrainian-flag:** ウクライナ国旗の	**medical-supply:** 医療用品の	**client:** 顧客
	Molotov cocktail: 火炎瓶		

■ ナチュラル音声のアクセント

カナダ英語

■ ニュースのミニ知識

戦禍に苦しむウクライナを支援する方法は、兵器を供給することだけではないことを、一般の企業、それも一玩具メーカーが示した。米国のCitizen Brickは、シカゴで「LEGO」ブロックのミニフィギュアやカスタム商品を販売している会社。同社は今回発売した商品の売り上げを、現在ウクライナで、難民や前線に医薬品を供給する活動をしている慈善団体に寄付したのである。一連の寄付に関して、同社は購入者に「世界一の顧客だ」と感謝を述べている。ちなみに最後のvery special clients in Ukraineとはウクライナにいる子供たちのことである。

■ Businessのミニ知識

Citizen Brickは当初、16,540米ドル（約200万円）を売り上げ、全額をこの慈善団体に寄付した。さらに同社は寄付額の目標として100,000米ドル（約1,200万円）を掲げ、新たにゼレンスキー大統領のミニフィギュアを発売。同年3月17日午後の時点で既に完売している。同社の素晴らしいアイデアがいかに人々の支持を得たかを表しており、この姿勢が将来のビジネスチャンスに繋がることも想像に難くない。

Words & Phrases（海外支援に関連した言葉）

□ Non-Governmental Organizations（NGO）	□ 非政府組織
□ Non-Profit Organization（NPO）	□ 非営利組織
□ peace building	□ 平和構築
□ post-conflict assistance; reconstruction assistance	□ 復興支援
□ stakeholder	□ 利害関係者
□ fund-raising activity	□ 募金活動
□ humanitarian assistance	□ 人道的援助
□ technical cooperation	□ 技術協力
□ Organization for Economic Cooperation and Development（OECD）	□ 経済協力開発機構
□ Japan International Cooperation Agency（JICA）	□ 国際協力機構

■ Let's Think!

さまざまな海外支援の取り組みについて、自分なりの意見や考えを英語で（難しければ日本語で）まとめてみよう。

Unit 2: 最新iOSで、マスクしたままロック解除！

🔊 Listen and check the words ❶

ナチュラル音声 🎧 05

Listen two times to the news read at natural speed. Check the box for each of the keywords below when you hear them, and look at the definition of each word to understand the news.

definition
- ☐ release [rɪ'lis] : to make a product available on the market
- ☐ update [ʌp'deɪt] : to bring something up to date by adding new information or making changes
- ☐ download ['daʊn,loʊd] : to transfer computer software or information from the internet to a computer
- ☐ previously ['priviəsli] : before the present time
- ☐ prompt [prɑmpt] : to urge (someone) into action

🔊 Listen and check the words ❷

ゆっくり音声[ポーズなし] 🎧 07

Listen two times to the same news read at slow speed without pauses. Check the box for each of the words or phrases below when you hear them, and write down any other information or expressions you hear.

- ☐ make sure
- ☐ swipe up
- ☐ PIN code
- ☐ Face ID
- ☐ multiple times

Notes

💡 Check your comprehension

What is the news about?

Headline

Choose the best headline for this news.

(A) Biometric Authentication Market Expected to Grow

(B) Is Face ID Better than Other Identification Systems?

(C) How to Unlock Your iPhone

(D) Face ID Updated for Mask Wearers

Check the transcript and make sure you understand the content. Then listen to the news again and again until you catch all of it.

Face ID Updated for Mask Wearers

Apple has released a new iPhone-software update, iOS 13.5, and you're going to want to make sure you download this one. They made it much easier to unlock your iPhone when wearing a mask. When mask-wearing users swipe up, they can immediately input their PIN code. Previously, Face ID would try to recognize your face multiple times before prompting for your PIN.

Aired on May 22, 2020

TOEIC-style Questions

1. What was released?

(A) A new facial recognition system that can work with mask-wearers

(B) Various types of biometric authentication

(C) Simple and speedy downloadable apps for mask-wearers

(D) A new alert indicating whether mask wearing is needed

2. What does iOS 13.5 enable the user to do?

(A) To swipe up the screen faster than its previous model

(B) To input the PIN code with one movement

(C) To download information on masks

(D) To unlock the screen, even with a mask on

Use this page to practice slash listening and shadowing. Circle the subject and underline the verb to understand subject-verb agreement.

最新 iOS で、マスクしたまま口ック解除！

Apple has released a new iPhone-software update, /

iOS 13.5, /

and you're going to want to make sure you download this one. //

They made it much easier to unlock your iPhone /

when wearing a mask. //

When mask-wearing users swipe up, /

they can immediately input their PIN code. //

Previously, /

Face ID would try to recognize your face multiple times /

before prompting for your PIN. //

語注

update: ① 〜をアップデートする ② アップデート、更新 **wearer:** 着用者 **release:** 〜を発売する、配信開始する **want to do:** 《話》…した方がいい	**make sure(that):** 確実に〜となるようにする **download:** 〜をダウンロードする **unlock:** 〜のロックを解除する **mask-wearing:** マスクを着用している	**swipe up:** （画面を）上方向にスワイプする **immediately:** 即座に **input:** 〜を入力する **PIN:** 暗証番号 ▶personal identification number の略	**previously:** 以前は **recognize:** 〜を認識する、認証する **multiple times:** 複数回 **prompt:** 促す

■ ナチュラル音声のアクセント

オーストラリア英語

■ ニュースのミニ知識

IT技術のめざましい発展により、ビジネスや日常生活はますます便利になっているが、情報漏えいや不正アクセスなど、セキュリティ上の問題も深刻になっている。そのため、セキュリティの強化のために多要素認証(本人確認の手段として、性質の異なる複数の要素の組み合わせを用いる認証方式)が導入されるケースが多くなっている。その中でもよく使われるユーザー固有の身体的特徴に基づく生体認証(biometric authentication)には、指紋(fingerprinting)、網膜(retina)や虹彩(iris)、静脈(vein)など、様々な種類がある。スマホでは今回のニュースで取り上げられている顔認証(Face ID)の他、指紋認証(Touch ID)も画面のロック解除に頻繁に使用されている。

■ Businessのミニ知識

iOSとは、アップル社が開発および提供しているオペレーティングシステムであり、iPhone, iPod touch iPad等に搭載されている。つまり、iPhoneやiPadを動かすためのプログラムである。2007年にリリースされたiPhone OS 1(アイフォーン オーエス ワン)以来、毎年のように更新されている。アップル社はiPhoneに搭載されるオペレーティングシステムの正式名称を「iPhone OS」から2010年に「iOS」に改称した。2023年時点で、最新バージョンはiOS 16.5である。

Words & Phrases(生体認証に関連した言葉)

□ authentication	□ 認証、証明
□ biometric authentication	□ 生体認証
□ fingerprint recognition	□ 指紋認識
□ iris recognition	□ 虹彩認識
□ retinal scan	□ 網膜スキャン　cf. retina authentication 網膜認証
□ voice recognition	□ 音声認識
□ vein pattern-recognition	□ 静脈認証
□ behavioral biometrics	□ 行動的生体認証

■ Let's Think!

様々な生体認証の長所・欠点を調べて、英語で(難しければ日本語で)まとめてみよう。

Unit 3: 米民間宇宙船　有人音速飛行で宇宙空間へ

🔊 Listen and check the words ❶

ナチュラル音声

Listen two times to the news read at natural speed. Check the box for each of the keywords below when you hear them, and look at the definition of each word to understand the news.

definition
- ☐ roar　　　[rɔːʳ]　　　: a loud continuous noise made by a machine
- ☐ milestone　[maɪlstoʊn]　: a very important event in the development of something
- ☐ leap　　　[liːp]　　　: very fast progress
- ☐ quest　　　[kwest]　　: a long search for something
- ☐ soar　　　[sɔːʳ]　　　: to rise quickly into the air

🔊 Listen and check the words ❷

ゆっくり音声[ポーズなし]

Listen two times to the same news read at slow speed without pauses. Check the box for each of the words or phrases below when you hear them, and write down any other information or expressions you hear.

- ☐ billionaire
- ☐ test flight
- ☐ craft
- ☐ passenger plane
- ☐ reach the edge of

Notes

💡 Check your comprehension

What is the news about?

Headline

Choose the best headline for this news.

(A) A Trip to Space

(B) Taking Tourists to Space

(C) Passenger Plane Reaches the Moon

(D) Virgin Galactic Tests Spaceplane

Check the transcript and make sure you understand the content. Then listen to the news again and again until you catch all of it.

Virgin Galactic Tests Spaceplane

That is the roar of rocket engines that launched billionaire Richard Branson's Virgin Galactic [on] a giant leap forward in its quest to take tourists into space. The craft soared more than 50 miles, or 80 kilometers, above the Earth's surface in yet another test flight. Virgin's supersonic plane, the *VSS Unity*, touched the outer limits of Earth's atmosphere on Thursday in a milestone move above the Mojave Desert. This is the first time the passenger plane has reached the edge of space.

Aired on December 14, 2018

TOEIC-style Questions

1. According to the article, which of the following is most likely true?
   (A) Richard Branson successfully flew into space.
   (B) Virgin's spaceplane touched the edge of space.
   (C) Passenger planes have reached the edge of space before.
   (D) The roar of rocket engines reached space.

2. What was the purpose for developing the spaceplane?
   (A) To investigate how far the spaceplane can reach.
   (B) To learn about the universe for developing new technology.
   (C) To collect data in space.
   (D) To take tourists into space.

Use this page to practice slash listening and shadowing. Circle the subject and underline the verb to understand subject-verb agreement.

米民間宇宙船
有人音速飛行で宇宙空間へ

ACE TOURISM?

SUPERSONIC PLANE REACHES OUTER LIMITS

CNN NEWSROC

That is the roar of rocket engines/
that launched billionaire Richard Branson's Virgin Galactic/
[on] a giant leap forward/
in its quest to take tourists into space.//
The craft soared/
more than 50 miles, or 80 kilometers, above the Earth's surface/
in yet another test flight.//
Virgin's supersonic plane, the *VSS Unity*,/
touched the outer limits of Earth's atmosphere/
on Thursday/
in a milestone move above the Mojave Desert.//
This is the first time/
the passenger plane has reached the edge of space.//

語注

test: 〜をテストする、試験する	**quest to do:** 〜しようとする努力	**test flight:** 試験飛行	**Mojave Desert:** モハーヴェ砂漠 ▶米南西部に広がる砂漠
spaceplane: 宇宙飛行機	**craft:** 航空機、宇宙船	**supersonic plane:** 超音速機	**passenger plane:** 旅客機
launch A on B: A(人や新製品など)をB(道のりや世界)に乗り出させる、送り出す	**soar:** 飛翔(ひしょう)する、空高く飛ぶ	**outer limits:** 外縁	**reach the edge of:** 〜の端、縁、へりに到達する
	yet another: さらにもう一度の	**atmosphere:** 大気圏	
		milestone: 画期的な、歴史的な	

■ ナチュラル音声のアクセント

アメリカ英語

■ ニュースのミニ知識

Virgin Galacticは宇宙旅行のチケットを45万ドル（約6700万円）で販売している（UchuBiz, 2022）。民間人が日常生活の中で宇宙に行ける日がくるのもそう遠くないかもしれない。機会があれば、あなたは行ってみたいと思う？　Virgin Galacticの創業者はリチャード・ブランソンで、イギリスの実業家である。Virgin Recordの産みの親で、航空事業で成功し、鉄道、映画館、金融、飲料水などあらゆるものに挑戦し、Virgin Groupという大きなグループを作り上げている。これほどの大きなグループをつくりあげた人物は世界に類をみない。起業家を志す人は、彼の自伝を読んでみたり、インタビューを聞いてみたりすれば、教訓が得られるかも知れない。

■ Businessのミニ知識

Virgin Groupの会長のブランソン氏は、冒険家としても有名で、過去に気球で大陸横断を試みている。その時に死んでもおかしくない経験をしているが、その後も、何度も気球での世界一周を試みている（吉成、2014）。あるインタビュー記事で、起業家と冒険家であることは似ていると言い、どちらもサバイバルの問題だと。起業家ならビジネスが生き残るように、冒険家なら自分が生き残れるようにと。今年、この記事を思い出させる出来事があった。ブランソン氏は、2017年にVirgin Orbitという民間の宇宙開発企業も創設していたが、Virgin Orbitは失敗に終わり、2023年4月に連邦倒産法第11章の適用を申請し、破綻した。しかし、その後Virgin Orbitの資産を約24億円で売っている（UchuBiz, 2023）。ブランソン氏は、ヴァージンはグループとして強くなったと思うとインタビューで話していた。一つの会社が破綻しても、他の数百の会社があるので、彼のビジネスは残り、彼のミッションはこれからも終わることはないだろう。

Words & Phrases（宇宙産業に関連した言葉）

□ R & D（Research & Development）　□ 研究開発

□ technological innovation　　　□ 技術革新

□ investment　　　　　　　　　　□ 投資

□ industrial competitiveness　　□ 産業競争力

□ industrial relations　　　　　　□ 産業関係

□ International Space Station（ISS）　□ 国際宇宙ステーション

□ aerospace industry　　　　　　□ 航空宇宙産業

□ venture companies　　　　　　□ ベンチャー企業

□ space tourism　　　　　　　　　□ 宇宙観光事業

■ Let's Think!

民間人の宇宙旅行について、自分なりの意見や考えを英語で（難しければ日本語で）まとめてみよう。

Listen and check the words ❶

Listen two times to the news read at natural speed. Check the box for each of the keywords below when you hear them, and look at the definition of each word to understand the news.

☐ investigation   [ɪnˌvɛstɪˈɡeɪʃən] : an examination of the facts about a situation
☐ conduct   [kəndʌkt]   : to do a particular activity
☐ health effect   [helθ ɪfekt]   : health impact; a change in health caused by something
☐ exhaust fumes   [ɪɡzɔːst fjuːmz] : waste gases that come out of a vehicle, or a machine
☐ diesel fuel   [diːzˀl fjuːəl]   : a type of oil used as a fuel instead of gasoline

Listen and check the words ❷

Listen two times to the same news read at slow speed without pauses. Check the box for each of the words or phrases below when you hear them, and write down any other information or expressions you hear.

☐ call for
☐ hire
☐ be intended to do
☐ carcinogenic
☐ unjustifiable

Notes

💡 Check your comprehension

What is the news about?

Headline

Choose the best headline for this news.

(A) Carcinogenic Fuel Used in Auto Tests
(B) Monkeys Used in Auto Tests
(C) Humans Used in Auto Tests
(D) Robots Used in Auto Tests

Check the transcript and make sure you understand the content. Then listen to the news again and again until you catch all of it.

Monkeys Used in Auto Tests

Volkswagen's supervisory board is calling for an investigation into the use of monkeys to test the health effects of diesel exhaust fumes. The *New York Times* reports three German carmakers—Volkswagen, Daimler and BMW—hired researchers to conduct the tests. The research was intended to show that modern diesel fuel is safe and not carcinogenic. A German newspaper also reported the same researchers conducted studies of exhaust fumes on people. The German government said the research was unjustifiable.

Aired on January 30, 2018

TOEIC-style Questions

1. Who is asking for an investigation of the test?

(A) The supervisory board of Volkswagen

(B) Three German automakers

(C) A German media group

(D) The German government

2. What was the purpose of the auto tests?

(A) To show that the modern diesel fuel is still toxic.

(B) To develop cars that monkeys can drive.

(C) To investigate the health effects of exhaust fumes on humans.

(D) To demonstrate that anyone can conduct the auto test.

Use this page to practice slash listening and shadowing. Circle the subject and underline the verb to understand subject-verb agreement.

独自動車３社がサルに
排ガス吸引実験

CARMAKERS UNDER FIRE FOR EMISSIONS STUDI

Volkswagen's supervisory board is calling for an investigation/
into the use of monkeys to test the health effects of diesel
exhaust fumes.//
The *New York Times* reports/ three German carmakers—/
Volkswagen, Daimler and BMW—/
hired researchers to conduct the tests.//
The research was intended/
to show that modern diesel fuel is safe and not carcinogenic.//
A German newspaper also reported/
the same researchers conducted studies of exhaust fumes
on people.//
The German government said/
the research was unjustifiable.//

Unit
4

語注

auto: =automobile 自動車の	**health effect:** 健康面への影響	**hire:** 〜を雇う	**diesel fuel:** ディーゼル燃料
supervisory board: 監査役会	**diesel:** ディーゼル	**conduct:** (調査・研究などを)行う、実施する	**carcinogenic:** 発がん性の
call for: 〜を要求する、求める	**exhaust fumes:** 排ガス	**be intended to do:** 〜することを目的としている	**study:** 研究
investigation into: 〜についての調査	**carmaker:** 自動車メーカー		**unjustifiable:** 容認できない、弁解のできない

■ ナチュラル音声のアクセント

オーストラリア英語

■ ニュースのミニ知識

自動車は便利な移動の道具である。便利だが、便利なものには負の面もある。2015年にホルクスワーゲン（VW）のディーゼルエンジンにおける排ガス不正が発覚して以来、大手自動車の不正疑惑が相次いだ。健康よりも経済が優先されたのだろうか。自動車からである排ガスには、健康被害をもたらす有害物質が含まれる。平均的な大型ディーゼル車トラックが、1km走行したときに排出するすす（粒子状物質）の量は約1グラムである。このすすを人が吸い込むと、微粒子が肺の奥に入り込み、呼吸器系疾患を引き起こす。東京都内では、一日、約12トン排出されていることが分かった（東京都環境局、2018）。1999年東京都は「ディーゼル車NO作戦」を展開し、クリーンディーゼル車が普及した。クリーンディーゼル車は、約30%のCO_2排出削減が見込まれると国は補助金制度を設けてきたが、2023年4月1日以降対象から外れた。

■ Business のミニ知識

日本は、2020年10月、2050年カーボンニュートラルを目指すことを宣言し、ゼロエミッション・ビーグルの普及に取り組んでいる。ゼロエミッション・ビーグルとは、走行時に二酸化炭素などの排出ガスを出さない電気自動車やプラグインハイブリッド車のことである。乗用車に関しては、2035年までに新車販売で電動車100%実現を目指す（東京都環境局、2023）。2023年4月1日以降のクリーンディーゼル車への補助金は終了し、電気自動車やプラグインハイブリッド車が補助金の対象になっている（経済産業省、2023）。令和4年度補正予算案額700億円。ゼロエミッション・ビーグル用の電気がどのように、どこから発電されるかも気になるところだ。

Words & Phrases （自動車産業に関連する言葉）

□ assembly line   □ 流れ作業、組み立てライン

□ EV (Electric Vehicle)   □ 電気自動車

□ automakers   □ 自動車製造業者

□ autonomous driving   □ 自動運転

□ corporation   □ 法人

□ climate change   □ 気候変動

□ regulation   □ 規制

□ consumers   □ 消費者

■ Let's Think!

未来の自動車の在り方について、自分なりの意見や考えを英語で（難しければ日本語で）まとめてみよう。

Unit 5: マスク氏、メディア評価サイトを立ち上げ!?

🔊)) Listen and check the words ❶

ナチュラル音声 ‖14‖

Listen two times to the news read at natural speed. Check the box for each of the keywords below when you hear them, and look at the definition of each word to understand the news.

definition

☐ quote   [kwoʊt]   : to repeat what someone has said or written
☐ tweet   [twit]   : a short remark or piece of information posted on Twitter
☐ threaten   ['θret·ən]   : to suggest a threat of harm or damage
☐ rate   [reɪt]   : to judge the value of someone or something according to a particular scale
☐ credibility   [krɛdɪ'bɪlɪti]   : the extent to which someone is worthy of trust

🔊)) Listen and check the words ❷

ゆっくり音声[ポーズなし] ‖16‖

Listen two times to the same news read at slow speed without pauses. Check the box for each of the words or phrases below when you hear them, and write down any other information or expressions you hear.

☐ attacks against
☐ the media
☐ took aim at
☐ the press
☐ growing concern over

Notes

Check your comprehension

What is the news about?

Headline

Choose the best headline for this news.

(A) The Donald Trump of Silicon Valley

(B) Elon Musk Unhappy with News Media

(C) The Credibility of Journalism

(D) Concern over Elon Musk Growing

Check the transcript and make sure you understand the content. Then listen to the news again and again until you catch all of it.

Elon Musk Unhappy with News Media

A *New York Times* reporter is calling Tesla CEO Elon Musk, quote, "the Donald Trump of Silicon Valley" after his recent attacks against the media. And here's the tweet that started it all. Now, Elon Musk—he took aim at the press by threatening to create a site where the public can rate the credibility of every journalist. The billionaire—he was at it again over the weekend, calling newsrooms, quote, "bleak." Musk's attacks come amid growing concern over production problems at Tesla.

Aired on May 29, 2018

TOEIC-style Questions

1. What do Musk and Trump have in common?
   (A) Having production facilities in Silicon Valley
   (B) Having production problems at Tesla
   (C) Harshly attacking the media
   (D) Rating credibility of every journalist

2. What is the purpose of creating a new site?
   (A) To allow the public to evaluate the credibility of journalists
   (B) To allow the public to praise the news media
   (C) To criticize billionaires in the realm of journalists
   (D) To avoid criticism of Tesla's production problems

Transcript divided by slashes

ゆっくり音声［ポーズ入り］ 🎧 15

Use this page to practice slash listening and shadowing.
Circle the subject and underline the verb to understand
subject-verb agreement.

マスク氏、メディア評価サイトを 立ち上げ!?

MUSK VS MEDIA

MUSK THREATENS TO LAUNCH SITE THAT RATE

A *New York Times* reporter/

is calling Tesla CEO Elon Musk, quote, "the Donald Trump
of Silicon Valley"/

after his recent attacks against the media.//

And here's the tweet that started it all.//

Now, Elon Musk—/

he took aim at the press/

by threatening to create a site where the public can rate the
credibility of every journalist.//

The billionaire—/

he was at it again over the weekend,/

calling newsrooms, quote, "bleak."//

Musk's attacks come/

amid growing concern over production problems at Tesla.//

Unit
5

語注

(be)unhappy with: 〜に不満である **Tesla:** テスラ ▶米電気自動 車メーカー大手 **quote:** 引用始め	**take aim at:** 〜を狙う、〜に照準を 合わせる **threaten to do:** 〜すると脅す **site:** = website **the public:** 一般の人々、大衆	**rate:** 〜を格付けする、評価 する **credibility:** 信頼性、信ぴょう性、 真実性 **newsroom:** (新聞社・放送局の) ニュース編集室	**bleak:** 暗い、希望のない **amid growing concern over:** 〜への懸念が高まる中 で

■ ナチュラル音声のアクセント

アメリカ英語

■ ニュースのミニ知識

イーロン・マスク氏は2018年5月24日、一般の人々が記事の真実性を格付けでき、かつ各ジャーナリスト、編集者、出版社の信頼性のスコアを可視化するようなサイトを作ろうと思うという趣旨のツイートを発信した。マスク氏はそのサイト名を「Pravda」(プラウダ)と名付けるつもりだと述べている。Pravdaとはロシア語で「真実、正義」を意味する。

■ Businessのミニ知識

ドナルド・ジョン・トランプ氏(Donald John Trump)は、アメリカ合衆国の政治家、実業家。2017年1月20日 から2021年 1月20日まで第45代アメリカ合衆国大統領に在任した。イーロン・マスク氏はしばしば既存メディアとの対決姿勢を鮮明にしてきたが、トランプ氏も、大統領選の時期から自身に批判的な既存メディア、特に自身と敵対する有力メディア(CNNはその急先鋒)に対して「フェイクニュース」という言葉を使って攻撃を繰り返してきた。

Words & Phrases (SNSに関する言葉)

□ SNS (Social Networking Service) □ ソーシャルネットワーキングサービス

□ sign up □ 登録する

□ post □ 投稿する

□ create a profile □ プロフィールを作る

□ membership □ 会員(制)

□ share content □ コンテンツを共有する

□ interact with others □ 他人と交流する

□ (electronic) bulletin board service □ 電子掲示板サービス

■ Let's Think!

ツイート(tweet)などのSNSの長所・短所に関して、英語で(難しければ日本語で)まとめてみよう。

Unit 6: 金融大手シティの女性賃金は男性の99%

🔊 Listen and check the words ❶

ナチュラル音声 🎧 17

Listen two times to the news read at natural speed. Check the box for each of the keywords below when you hear them, and look at the definition of each word to understand the news.

definition
- ☐ parity ['pærətii] : the state of having equal pay or status
- ☐ reveal [rɪ'vil] : to make something known to somebody; disclose
- ☐ coworker ['kou,wɜːrkər] : a person that somebody works with
- ☐ factor ['fæktər] : one of several things that cause or influence something
- ☐ function ['fʌŋkʃən] : a special activity or purpose of a person or thing

🔊 Listen and check the words ❷

 ゆっくり音声[ポーズなし] 🎧 19

Listen two times to the same news read at slow speed without pauses. Check the box for each of the words or phrases below when you hear them, and write down any other information or expressions you hear.

- ☐ gauge A at B
- ☐ gender pay gap
- ☐ quest for
- ☐ shrouded in secrecy
- ☐ adjusted for

Notes

Check your comprehension

What is the news about?

Headline

Choose the best headline for this news.

(A) A Wall Street Bank in the US

(B) Citigroup Raises Gender Problems

(C) Citigroup Gauges Gender Pay Gap at 1%

(D) Citigroup Becomes the First Big Bank

Check the transcript and make sure you understand the content. Then listen to the news again and again until you catch all of it.

Citigroup Gauges Gender Pay Gap at 1%

In the quest for gender parity at work, pay has remained one of the issues most shrouded in secrecy. However, Citigroup has become the first big Wall Street bank to reveal its pay gap. It says its female workers in the US, Germany and the UK are paid 99 percent of what their male coworkers earn. The results have been adjusted for factors including job function, level and location. And Citigroup says it is working to close the pay gap that remains.

Aired on January 17, 2018

TOEIC-style Questions

1. According to the passage, how much do the female workers of Citigroup earn?

   (A) 99% of the male coworkers' pay before adjustment of some factors

   (B) 99% of the male coworkers' pay after adjustment of some factors

   (C) Depends on where they live

   (D) Not mentioned

2. What factors have adjusted the results?

   (A) Place of work

   (B) Position in the bank

   (C) Job function

   (D) All of the above

Use this page to practice slash listening and shadowing. Circle the subject and underline the verb to understand subject-verb agreement.

金融大手シティの
女性賃金は男性の99%

ROUP REVEALS 1% GENDER PAY GA

In the quest for gender parity at work, /

pay has remained one of the issues most shrouded in secrecy.//

However, /

Citigroup has become the first big Wall Street bank/

to reveal its pay gap.//

It says/

its female workers in the US, Germany and the UK/

are paid 99 percent of what their male coworkers earn.//

The results have been adjusted/

for factors including job function, level and location.//

And Citigroup says/

it is working to close the pay gap that remains.//

語注

gauge A at B: AをB(数値など)と測定する、算出する	**(be)shrouded in:** ～に覆われている、包まれている	**results:** (研究・調査などの)結果	**work to do:** ～すべく尽力する、努める
gender pay gap: 性差による賃金格差	**secrecy:** 秘密の状態、内密	**adjust A for B:** Bに応じてAを調整する	**close a gap:** 差を埋める、縮める
quest for: ～を求めること	**coworker:** 同僚	**function:** 役目、職務	
gender parity: 男女平等	**earn:** ～を稼ぐ、得る		

■ ナチュラル音声のアクセント

カナダ英語

■ ニュースのミニ知識

シティグループは1890年代までには米国最大の銀行、世界最大のクレジットカード発行体となり、1929年には世界最大の商業銀行となったが、その後サブプライム（住宅購入用途向け）ローン問題やリーマンショックでの金融危機によって経営は悪化し、事業を縮小している。シティによる男女間の賃金格差開示は、投資家らの間における企業経営陣の多様性向上を求める声の高まりという現状を反映している。資産運用世界最大手のブラックロックはこの前年に投資先の企業に対し、少なくとも女性2人を役員に登用するよう要求していたのだ。シティはこれを受けて、利益面や優秀な人材の保持という側面を考慮して女性やマイノリティの給与を増やしたのである。

■ Businessのミニ知識

男性賃金の中央値を100とした場合の女性賃金の中央値によって男女間の賃金格差を調べてみると、OECD（経済協力開発機構）での平均は88.4となっている。一方、日本は77.5であり、世界38か国が加盟するOECDの平均値に比べると、国際的にみて我が国の男女間賃金格差は大きいと言えるだろう。厚生労働省は2022年、この格差の解消に向けて女性活躍推進法に関する制度を改正し「男女の賃金の差異」の情報公表を必須項目とした。（常時雇用の労働者が301人以上の事業主対象）

Words & Phrases（男女格差に関連した言葉）

□ labor market	□ 労働市場
□ work-life balance	□ ワーク・ライフ・バランス
□ reproductive health	□ リプロダクティブ・ヘルス & ライツ（性と生殖に関する健康と権利）
□ empowerment	□ エンパワーメント
□ gender bias	□ ジェンダーバイアス
□ sexual harassment	□ セクハラ
□ abuse of authority	□ パワハラ
□ social role; social function	□ 社会的役割
□ Equal Employment Act	□ 男女雇用機会均等法
□ positive（affirmative）action	□ ポジティブ・アクション（＝アファーマティブ・アクション）

■ Let's Think!

日本における男女格差について、自分なりの意見や考えを英語で（難しければ日本語で）まとめてみよう。

Unit 7: H&M、人種差別表現の広告で謝罪

Listen and check the words ❶

ナチュラル音声 [20]

Listen two times to the news read at natural speed. Check the box for each of the keywords below when you hear them, and look at the definition of each word to understand the news.

definition
- ☐ criticize [krɪtɪsaɪz] : to say that you think somebody/something is bad or wrong
- ☐ racist [reɪsɪst] : having the belief that some races of people are better than others
- ☐ hoodie [hʊdɪ] : a sweatshirt with a hood
- ☐ apology [əpɒlədʒi] : words saying sorry for doing something wrong
- ☐ horribly ['hɒrɪblɪ] : in a way that is very bad

Listen and check the words ❷

ゆっくり音声[ポーズなし] [22]

Listen two times to the same news read at slow speed without pauses. Check the box for each of the words or phrases below when you hear them, and write down any other information or expressions you hear.

- ☐ clothing retailer
- ☐ issue an apology
- ☐ insensitive
- ☐ blatantly
- ☐ backlash

Notes

Unit 7

Check your comprehension

What is the news about?

Headline

Choose the best headline for this news.

(A) Coolest Monkey in the Jungle

(B) Backlash from Social Media

(C) H&M Criticized for "Racist" Hoodie

(D) Collaborating with Clothing Retailer

Check the transcript and make sure you understand the content. Then listen to the news again and again until you catch all of it.

H&M Criticized for "Racist" Hoodie

Clothing retailer H&M has issued an extensive apology for a horribly insensitive ad many are calling blatantly racist. It shows a little black boy in a green hoodie with the phrase "Coolest Monkey in the Jungle." After social media lit up, H&M pulled the image and also the hoodie from its stores, but the backlash continues. Singer The Weeknd tweeted that he would no longer be working with the retailer. He had collaborated with the fashion line in 2017.

Aired on January 10, 2018

TOEIC-style Questions

1. According to the article, which of the following is true?
   (A) H&M was criticized for forcing overwork.
   (B) H&M carefully chose the phrase for the hoodie.
   (C) H&M intentionally issued a racist ad.
   (D) H&M expressed an apology for the ad.

2. According to the singer, The Weeknd, which of the following is most likely to happen?
   (A) He will be singing for H&M.
   (B) He will stop working with H&M.
   (C) He will be collaborating with other singers.
   (D) He will be apologizing on behalf of H&M.

Use this page to practice slash listening and shadowing. Circle the subject and underline the verb to understand subject-verb agreement.

H&M、人種差別表現の広告で謝罪

Printed hooded top
£7.99

Clothing retailer H&M has issued an extensive apology/
for a horribly insensitive ad/
many are calling blatantly racist.//
It shows a little black boy in a green hoodie/
with the phrase "Coolest Monkey in the Jungle."//
After social media lit up,/
H&M pulled the image/
and also the hoodie from its stores,/
but the backlash continues.//
Singer The Weeknd tweeted/
that he would no longer be working with the retailer.//
He had collaborated with the fashion line in 2017.//

語注

criticize A for B:	**clothing retailer:**	**insensitive:**	**backlash:**
AをBを理由に批判する	衣料品業者	（言葉などが）無神経な	反動、反発
racist:	**issue an apology:**	**ad:** = advertisement	**work with:**
人種差別的な	謝罪声明を出す	宣伝、広告	〜と提携する
hoodie:	**extensive:**	**blatantly:**	**collaborate with:**
パーカー　▶フード付	詳細に及ぶ	露骨に、明らかに	〜と協力する、コラボ
きスウェットシャツ	**horribly:**	**light up:**	レーションする
	ひどく	火がつく	**fashion line:**
			ファッションブランド

■ ナチュラル音声のアクセント

オーストラリア英語

■ ニュースのミニ知識

緑のパーカーを着たモデルの母親はこの広告がメディアに出ると、自分の子供をお金のために売ったと批判に晒された。インタビューで、このパーカーは人によっては気分を害するものであったかも知れないが、彼女にとっては人種差別的ではなかった、どちらの意見も尊重されるべきだ、と応えている（BBC, 2018）。ニュースのタイトルのダブルクオーテーションマーク（" "）がついているが、これは "いわゆる、世に言われている" という意味を表しており、事実かどうかは別として、ソーシャルメディアではこのパーカーが人種差別的だとして批判されている、ということを表している。皆さんは、この広告に対してどう感じただろうか。

■ Businessのミニ知識

H&Mは、スウェーデンのアパレルメーカーで、アパレル業界の中で、ZARAに次いで世界で2番目に大きい。低価格でありながらファッション性の高い商品を扱うZARAやUNIQLOといったファストファッションの代表的なファッションブランドである。2021年12月〜22年5月期（上半期）決算では、売上高が前年同期と比べ、約2割増しの1036億7000万スウェーデンクローナ（約1兆3477億円）、純利益は2倍以上の38億9900万スウェーデンクローナ（約506億円）と増収増益だった（WWDJAPAN, 2023）。ファッション業界は売り上げを上げるために有名なアーティストとコラボをするが、アーティストの承認を得ずにアーティストの画像が入った商品を売り出していることもあり、よく問題になっている。2022年には、H&Mが歌手のジャスティン・ビーバーの承認なしに、商品を売り出したとして、ビーバーは自身のインスタグラムで、H&Mから出されている自分の商品は買わないようにとファンに訴えていた。

Words & Phrases（ファッション産業に関連した言葉）

□ trend   □ 流行

□ manufacturing   □ 製造

□ distribution   □ 流通

□ marketing   □ マーケティング

□ advertising   □ 広告

□ capitalism   □ 資本主義

□ sustainable fashion   □ 衣服の生産から、着用、廃業に至るプロセスにおいて将来にわたり持続可能であることを目指す取り組みのこと

□ green washing   □ 環境配慮をしているように装いごまかすこと

■ Let's Think!

この広告について、もしくは、（身近にある）人種差別について自分なりの意見や考えを英語で（難しければ日本語で）まとめてみよう。

Unit 8: アップル、iCloudデータを中国企業に移行

 ))) **Listen and check the words ❶**

ナチュラル音声 ‖23‖

Listen two times to the news read at natural speed. Check the box for each of the keywords below when you hear them, and look at the definition of each word to understand the news.

definition
- ☐ **iCloud** [aɪklaʊd] : a cloud storage service from Apple
- ☐ **regulations** [regjʊleɪʃˀn(z)] : rules made by a government
- ☐ **register** [redʒɪstəˀ] : to put your name on an official list
- ☐ **state-run** [ˌsteɪtˈrʌn] : controlled by the government
- ☐ **unlock** [ʌnlɒk] : to open doors or containers using a key

))) **Listen and check the words ❷**

ゆっくり音声[ポーズなし] ‖25‖

Listen two times to the same news read at slow speed without pauses. Check the box for each of the words or phrases below when you hear them, and write down any other information or expressions you hear.

- ☐ mainland China
- ☐ put under Chinese control
- ☐ cave to
- ☐ has jurisdiction over
- ☐ as well as

Notes

Unit 8

Check your comprehension

What is the news about?

Headline

Choose the best headline for this news.

（A） No iCloud Account Registered in China

（B） Apple Paid Money for iCloud Data

（C） Apple Asks China to Unlock data

（D） iCloud Data Put under Chinese Control

Check the transcript and make sure you understand the content. Then listen to the news again and again until you catch all of it.

iCloud Data Put under Chinese Control

Well, Apple is the latest company to cave to China's cybersecurity regulations. Any iCloud account registered in mainland China is removed to state-run Chinese servers. Well, that means the Chinese government has jurisdiction over users' iCloud data, as well as the digital keys to unlock encrypted files. And it's making privacy advocates and human-rights groups very nervous.

Aired on February 28, 2018

TOEIC-style Questions

1. What happens to the iCloud accounts registered in mainland China?

   (A) They are taken away to Chinese servers.

   (B) The Chinese government has the right to control their iCloud data.

   (C) The Chinese government can open their encrypted files with the digital keys.

   (D) All of the above

2. What does the Chinese government jurisdiction over iCloud data do?

   (A) It protects privacy and human rights.

   (B) It makes people who care about privacy or human rights very nervous.

   (C) It makes business and economy run smooth.

   (D) It gets them more iCloud accounts.

Use this page to practice slash listening and shadowing. Circle the subject and underline the verb to understand subject-verb agreement.

アップル、iCloudデータを
中国企業に移行

Well, Apple is the latest company/

to cave to China's cybersecurity regulations.//

Any iCloud account registered in mainland China/

is removed to state-run Chinese servers.//

Well, that means/

the Chinese government has jurisdiction over users' iCloud data,/

as well as the digital keys to unlock encrypted files.//

And it's making privacy advocates and human-rights groups very nervous.//

Unit
8

語注

iCloud:	**register:**	～に対する管轄権を持　神経をとがらせている
▶アップル社が提供するクラウドサービス	～を登録する	つ
	mainland China:	**A as well as B:**
put...under someone's control:	中国	BだけではなくAも
…を～の管理下に置く	**remove A to B:**	
	AをBに移動させる	**encrypted:**
cave(in)to:		暗号化された
～に屈する、降参する	**state-run:**	**privacy advocate:**
	国営の	プライバシー保護推進
regulations:	**have jurisdiction**	者
法規、法令	**over:**	**nervous:**

■ ナチュラル音声のアクセント

オーストラリア英語

■ ニュースのミニ知識

アップル社の今回の動きは、中国が2017年6月に施行したサイバーセキュリティ法に準拠するための
ものである。この法律では、同国内でのクラウドサービスは、同国の企業によって運営され、そのデー
タは国内で保存される必要があると定められている。データの移行により、中国政府は、容易に国
内ユーザーのデータにアクセスできるようになった。

■ Business のミニ知識

iCloudとは、書類や写真、動画などを、アップル社が提供するクラウド上に保管して、ネットワーク
につながったPCやスマートフォン、タブレットなどの情報端末からアクセスできるようにするサービス
である。このようなクラウドサービスの利用において、情報の流失のおそれに至る事案が増加しており、
クラウドサービスの利用における最大のリスクとして社会的な問題になってきている。こうしたリスク
を抑えるために、セキュリティを維持する万全の仕組みが必要となってきている。

Words & Phrases（クラウドサービスに関連する言葉）

☐ cloud service   ☐ クラウドサービス

☐ login   ☐ ログイン

☐ password   ☐ パスワード、暗証番号

☐ device   ☐ デバイス

☐ SIM card   ☐ SIM カード（SIM=subscriber identity module）

☐ screen lock   ☐ 画面ロック

☐ user account   ☐ ユーザーアカウント

☐ hacking   ☐ 不正アクセス

☐ back up ones' data   ☐ データをバックアップしておく

■ Let's Think!

クラウドサービスにおける政府の介入について、自分なりの意見や考えを英語で（難しければ日本語
で）まとめてみよう。

Unit 9: ランボルギーニ、3年以内に全車種ハイブリッド化へ

Listen and check the words ❶

ナチュラル音声 | 26 |

Listen two times to the news read at natural speed. Check the box for each of the keywords below when you hear them, and look at the definition of each word to understand the news.

definition
☐ hybrid   [haɪbrɪd] : something that is the product of mixing two different things
☐ still   [stɪl] : despite what has just been said
☐ feel   [fil] : the impression that is created by a situation
☐ operate   [ɑpərˌeɪt] : to work in a particular way
☐ purely   [pjʊrli] : only, completely

Listen and check the words ❷

ゆっくり音声［ポーズなし］ | 28 |

Listen two times to the same news read at slow speed without pauses. Check the box for each of the words or phrases below when you hear them, and write down any other information or expressions you hear.

☐ go green
☐ plug-in hybrid
☐ internal-combustion engine
☐ at times
☐ fear not

Notes

Check your comprehension

What is the news about?

Headline

Choose the best headline for this news.

(A) New Lamborghinis to Be Released

(B) Green: Lamborghini's Most Popular Paint Color

(C) Lamborghinis: Pride of Italian Luxury Cars

(D) All Lamborghinis to Be Hybrid

Unit 9

Check the transcript and make sure you understand the content. Then listen to the news again and again until you catch all of it.

All Lamborghinis to Be Hybrid

Well, the Lamborghini is going green, and we don't mean the paint color. The Italian luxury-car maker says all of its new cars will be plug-in hybrids by the end of 2024. That means they will still have the feel and sound of an internal combustion engine but can also operate under purely electric power at times. So fear not, Lambo fans: they will still go fast and sound fast.

Aired on May 19, 2021

TOEIC-style Questions

1. What is the most important point this article is trying to make?

   (A) Expectations are high for environmentally friendly vehicles.

   (B) Lamborghini will be faster and more powerful.

   (C) A new type of Italian luxury cars will be released.

   (D) "Green" Lamborghinis will still keep their powerful features.

2. What will the maker sacrifice to achieve this point?

   (A) Its incomparable speed

   (B) Its vigorous sound

   (C) Its paint color

   (D) None of the above

Use this page to practice slash listening and shadowing. Circle the subject and underline the verb to understand subject-verb agreement.

ランボルギーニ、3年以内に 全車種ハイブリッド化へ

Well, the Lamborghini is going green, /
and we don't mean the paint color. //
The Italian luxury-car maker says /
all of its new cars will be plug-in hybrids /
by the end of 2024. //
That means /
they will still have the feel and sound of an internal combustion engine /
but can also operate under purely electric power at times. //
So fear not, Lambo fans: /
they will still go fast and sound fast. //

語注

Lamborghini: ランボルギーニ ▶イタリアの高級車メーカー、またその車 **hybrid:** 複数の動力源で動く、ハイブリッドの **go green:** 環境に配慮するようになる **paint color:** 塗装色	**luxury car:** 高級車 **plug-in hybrid:** プラグインハイブリッド車 ▶家庭用電源で電池を充電できるハイブリッド車 **by the end of:** 〜の終わりまでに **still:** それでも **feel:**	感触 **internal combustion engine:** 内燃エンジン **operate under electric power:** 電力で稼働する、電気で走る **purely:** 〜だけで、単に、もっぱら **at times:**	時々、時には **fear not:** 恐れるなかれ、心配無用 **Lambo:** ▶ランボルギーニの愛称 ■関連語・派生語 **emissions standards:** 排出基準

■ ナチュラル音声のアクセント

オーストラリア英語

■ ニュースのミニ知識

創業者であるフェルッチオ・ランボルギーニは、「レースには出ない」ことを社是としていた。これは当時F1に参戦していたあるメーカーが「レースを本業とし、市販車はそのための資金稼ぎと考え、ユーザーをないがしろにしていた」ことに反発したためとも言われているが定かではない。実際、1989年、エンジン供給の形でF1に参戦したが結果は振るわず、1993年にはF1を撤退している。なお鈴木亜久里が日本グランプリで日本人としてはじめて3位入賞を飾ったローラ・LC90もランボルギーニ製ユニットを搭載していた。

■ Business のミニ知識

創業者フェルッチオは、第二次大戦後、イタリアで軍のトラックを改造し民間に販売することで富を得て、のちに高性能なトラクターを自社開発して成功を収めた。優秀なメカニックでもあった彼は、所有するフェラーリが壊れやすいことに悩み、それを修理することをビジネスチャンスと捉え、高級車の世界に入っていった。ランボルギーニ400GTが発表される頃になると、独創性と快適性を両立させたスタイルはエグゼクティブの間で話題となり、この後1966年のランボルギーニ・ミウラ、1971年のランボルギーニ・カウンタックと有名な車を次々と送り出し、世界的スーパースポーツのブランドとなった。

Words & Phrases（環境保護に関連した言葉）

□ carbon dioxide	□ 二酸化炭素
□ pollution	□ 汚染
□ greenhouse gas	□ 温室効果ガス
□ Kyoto Protocol	□ 京都議定書
□ ecotourism	□ エコ・ツーリズム
□ renewable energy	□ 再生可能エネルギー
□ industrial waste	□ 産業廃棄物
□ ecosystem	□ 生態系
□ biodiversity	□ 生物多様性
□ decarbonization	□ 脱炭素

■ Let's Think!

環境に配慮したエネルギーに関わる技術や研究開発を調べて、英語で（難しければ日本語で）まとめてみよう。

Unit 10: 独特な動きで話題のロボット犬、販売開始

 Listen and check the words ❶

ナチュラル音声 29

Listen two times to the news read at natural speed. Check the box for each of the keywords below when you hear them, and look at the definition of each word to understand the news.

definition

☐ construction [kənstrʌkʃ°n] : the process of building something such as a bridge or a building

☐ lab [læb] : =laboratory, a room used for scientific research or experiments

☐ quadruped [kwɒdrʊped] : an animal that has four legs

☐ site [saɪt] : a place where something is being built

☐ spot [spɒt] : to give or lend a small amount of money

 Listen and check the words ❷

ゆっくり音声［ポーズなし］ 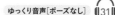 31

Listen two times to the same news read at slow speed without pauses. Check the box for each of the words or phrases below when you hear them, and write down any other information or expressions you hear.

☐ on sale
☐ dog-like machine
☐ their very own
☐ for the price of
☐ construction sites

Notes

Unit
10

Check your comprehension

What is the news about?

Headline

Choose the best headline for this news.

(A) Four-Legged Robot Now on Sale

(B) Dog-Like Robot Developed in Boston

(C) Quadruped Robot Earns $75,000

(D) Four-Legged Machine Runs Full Speed

Check the transcript and make sure you understand the content. Then listen to the news again and again until you catch all of it.

Four-Legged Robot Now on Sale

This is Spot. It's the famous robot quadruped, or four-legged dog-like machine, from Boston Dynamics. And now, American companies can buy their very own Spot for the price of $74,500. It has found uses in factories, research labs and construction sites. But the question is: Will someone spot $75,000 just to see Spot run?

Aired on June 18, 2020

TOEIC-style Questions

1. Who would be likely to buy the robot?
   (A) People who want to see their robot pets run a race
   (B) Workers at Boston Dynamics
   (C) Restaurants for dog lovers in the US
   (D) American construction companies

2. What information about Spot is likely to be new to the audience?
   (A) Its shape
   (B) Its developer
   (C) Its price
   (D) Its running speed

Use this page to practice slash listening and shadowing. Circle the subject and underline the verb to understand subject-verb agreement.

独特な動きで話題のロボット犬、販売開始

This is Spot.//
It's the famous robot quadruped,/
or four-legged dog-like machine,/
from Boston Dynamics.//
And now,/
American companies can buy their very own Spot/
for the price of $74,500.//
It has found uses/
in factories, research labs and construction sites.//
But the question is:/
Will someone spot $75,000/
just to see Spot run?//

Unit
10

語注

four-legged: 四足の、四つ足の **(be)on sale:** 販売されている **Spot:** ▶日本における「ポチ」 のような、米国の犬の典 型的な名前で、spotは 「斑(ぶち)」のこと	**quadruped:** 四足動物(quadr(i) 4つ の＋ped 足) **dog-like:** 犬のような **Boston Dynamics:** ▶米ロボット研究開発 企業	**one's very own:** 自分だけの、自分専用 の：veryは形容詞で「他 ならぬ、まさに」 **for the price of:** 〜という価格で **find a use in:** 〜において用いられる ようになる	**research lab:** 研究室 **construction site:** 建設現場 **spot(A)B:** (Aに) B(金額) を貸 す ▶ここではAが省 略され、「出す、払う」 の意味。名前のSpotと の掛け言葉になる

■ ナチュラル音声のアクセント

アメリカ英語

■ ニュースのミニ知識

Boston Dynamics は、ロボット工学と人工知能を組み合わせた新技術で、車輪走行が難しい雪道や斜面、瓦礫の散乱する災害現場や段差の多い悪路を、重い荷物を搭載して進む4足歩行型ロボットを開発してきた。2005年に開発された4足歩行の Big Dog は、軍事現場を想定した優れた機能も備えていたが、機能よりも、エンジン駆動による騒音と奇天烈な外観で一躍有名になった。改良を重ねた結果、今回取り上げられている Spot は、静音のモーター駆動で軽量化され、ユーザー個人の用途に合わせたプログラムの変更や遠隔操作が可能になり、瓦礫の散乱する災害現場や障害物の多い作業現場で利用できると言う。日本でも、すでに、竹中工務店や鹿島建設が実際に建築現場で利用しており、今後は民間での需要が期待されている。

■ Business のミニ知識

Boston Dynamics は、MIT（マサチューセッツ工科大学）の Marc Raibert 教授によって1992年に設立された。当初は、米軍の支援を受けて、軍用のトレーニングプログラム等を開発していたが、2013年に Google に買収されている。その後、数多くのユニークなロボットを開発するも、いずれも実用化や市販化に難点があり、短期的利益が出せず、2017年にはソフトバンクグループに売却される。さらに、2020年には、ソフトバンクも韓国の Hyundai Motor Group に80％の株式を売却した。Hyundai は、この買収により、世界最先端技術を携えてロボット事業に参入すると同時に、自律走行自動車や「空飛ぶ自動車」の電動垂直離着陸機（eVTOL）でも世界をリードすることが期待される。

Words & Phrases（ロボット産業に関連した言葉）

☐ biped	☐ 二足動物（bi（2）+ ped）
☐ centipede	☐ ムカデ（centi（百）+ ped）
☐（be）sold out	☐ 売り切れ、完売
☐（be）not for sale	☐ 非売品
☐ industrial robot	☐ 産業用ロボット
☐ military robot	☐ 軍事用ロボット
☐ educational robot	☐ 教育用ロボット
☐ android	☐ 人造人間
☐ robotic pet	☐ ロボット型ペット、ペットロボット

■ Let's Think!

ロボット産業について調べ、自分なりの意見や考えを英語で（難しければ日本語で）まとめてみよう。

Unit 11: 米シティグループ、初の女性CEO誕生へ

Listen and check the words ❶

ナチュラル音声 32

Listen two times to the news read at natural speed. Check the box for each of the keywords below when you hear them, and look at the definition of each word to understand the news.

definition

☐ CEO　　　　[si: i: oʊ]　: chief executive officer

☐ Wall Street　[wɔːl striːt]　: a street in New York where the Stock Exchange and major banks are

☐ Citigroup　　[sɪtigruːp]　: an American investment bank and financial services corporation

☐ lead　　　　 [liːd]　　　 : to be in control of ~

☐ join　　　　 [dʒɔɪn]　　 : to start work as an employee of a company

Listen and check the words ❷

ゆっくり音声[ポーズなし] 34

Listen two times to the same news read at slow speed without pauses. Check the box for each of the words or phrases below when you hear them, and write down any other information or expressions you hear.

☐ a piece of good news
☐ out of
☐ made history
☐ name Jane Fraser as
☐ is set to take over

Notes

Unit
11

💡 Check your comprehension

What is the news about?

Headline

Choose the best headline for this news.

(A) First Female CEO of *Wall Street Journal*

(B) First Female CEO of Major US Bank

(C) Citigroup Named Elon Musk as CEO

(D) First British CEO of Major US Bank

Check the transcript and make sure you understand the content. Then listen to the news again and again until you catch all of it.

First Female CEO of a Major US Bank

There was one piece of good news out of Wall Street Thursday. Citigroup has made history by naming Jane Fraser as its next CEO. I remind everyone it is 2020. She is the first woman to lead a major US bank. She's set to take over in February, about 16 years after she joined Citi.

Aired on September 11, 2020

TOEIC-style Questions

1. How many female CEOs were there in major US banks in 2020?

   (A) Zero

   (B) One

   (C) Two

   (D) Not mentioned

2. Why was Citigroup said to have made history?

   (A) By naming Jane Fraser as its next president

   (B) By deciding on a woman as its next CEO

   (C) By giving Jane Fraser the Best Mother Award

   (D) None of the above

Use this page to practice slash listening and shadowing.
Circle the subject and underline the verb to understand
subject-verb agreement.

米シティグループ、初の女性ＣＥＯ誕生へ

There was one piece of good news out of Wall Street/
Thursday.//
Citigroup has made history/
by naming Jane Fraser as its next CEO.//
I remind everyone/
it is 2020.//
She is the first woman/
to lead a major US bank.//
She's set to take over in February,/
about 16 years after she joined Citi.//

Unit
11

語注

CEO=chief executive officer: 最高経営責任者	Wall Street: ウォール街、米国金融市場	remind...(that): …に～ということを思い出させる、気づかせる	join: (組織に) 加わる、入る
major bank: 大手の銀行	Citigroup: 米大手金融会社シティグループ	lead: ～を率いる	■関連語・派生語 take the helm: かじを取る
a piece of good news: 朗報、いいニュース	make history: 歴史に残ることを成す	be set to do: ～することになっている	gender pay gap: 性別による賃金格差
out of: ～からの	name A as B: AをBに任命する	take over: 引き継ぐ、後継者となる	shareholder: 株主

■ ナチュラル音声のアクセント

カナダ英語

■ ニュースのミニ知識

米金融大手シティグループでは、スコットランド・セントアンドリューズ生まれのイギリス人ジェーン・フレイザー氏が、2021年2月、初の女性CEOとなった。フレイザー氏は、米ハーバード・ビジネス・スクールと英ケンブリッジ大学で学位を取得。ロンドンのゴールドマン・サックス、米コンサルタント会社マッキンゼーを経て、2004年にシティグループに入行した。以前のインタビューでは、アメリカでは女性にチャンスがあると感じて、アメリカに移住したと語っている。また2児の母でもあり、ワークライフバランスに関しても「同時に全てを手に入れることはできない」と述べ、2018年には米CNNのインタビューにおいて、自分がCEOになる可能性を否定していた。

■ Businessのミニ知識

「最高責任者" CEO"」と「社長 "president"」は異なる。アメリカの役職名で、CEOとは会社の中長期的な経営方針を決める経営陣の最高責任者を指し、「社長 "president"」とは、むしろ、経営方針に従って短期的な事業計画を実行する現場のトップを指す。したがって、役職としてはCEOの方が社長より上であるが、これらを兼任する場合もある。海外の有名なCEOには、イーロン・マスク（米国電気自動車会社テスラ、宇宙開発企業スペースX）、ダニエル・エク（音楽ストリーミングサービスSpotify）、マーク・ザッカーバーグ（Meta Platforms, Inc.(旧称Facebook, Inc.)）があげられる。

Words & Phrases（銀行や女性の社会進出に関連した言葉）

☐ bank employee	☐ 銀行員
☐ bank account	☐ 銀行口座
☐ ordinary deposit	☐ 普通預金
☐ fixed deposit	☐ 定期預金
☐ interest	☐ 利息
☐ online (internet) bank	☐ ネット銀行
☐ minority	☐ マイノリティ
☐ majority	☐ 多数派
☐ gender equality	☐ ジェンダー平等
☐ glass ceiling	☐ ガラスの天井

■ Let's Think!

日本においても企業や政府機関で働く女性が一定の職位以上に昇進できない傾向がみられるが、それについて、自分なりの意見を英語で（難しければ日本語で）まとめてみよう。

Unit 12: ついに着陸成功! スペース X の「スターシップ」

🔊))) Listen and check the words ❶

ナチュラル音声　🎧 35

Listen two times to the news read at natural speed. Check the box for each of the keywords below when you hear them, and look at the definition of each word to understand the news.

definition

☐ **prototype** [ˈproʊtətaɪp] : the original model on which other models based

☐ **nail** [neɪl] : to perform or complete something perfectly and impressively

☐ **launch** [lɔːntʃ] : to send something into space or into the sky

☐ **soar** [sɔːr] : to rise very quickly; to fly high up in the sky

☐ **descend** [dɪsend] : to move from a higher place to a lower place

🔊))) Listen and check the words ❷

ゆっくり音声[ポーズなし]　🎧 37

Listen two times to the same news read at slow speed without pauses. Check the box for each of the words or phrases below when you hear them, and write down any other information or expressions you hear.

☐ the first time ever
☐ landing pad
☐ launch vehicle
☐ of its kind
☐ stick it

Notes

💡 Check your comprehension

What is the news about?

Headline

Choose the best headline for this news.

(A) SpaceX's Starship Lands Successfully

(B) SpaceX's Starship First Launches for Mars

(C) SpaceX's Starship Soars Up 10 Km in Texas

(D) SpaceX Develops the Fifth Prototype

Unit
12

Check the transcript and make sure you understand the content. Then listen to the news again and again until you catch all of it.

SpaceX's Starship Lands Successfully

For the first time ever, SpaceX's Starship Mars prototype has nailed its landing. The SN15 rocket launched from south Texas Wednesday, soaring straight up 10 kilometers before descending safely onto a landing pad. It's the fifth spacecraft of its kind to attempt such a landing but the first to actually stick it. Starship is the launch vehicle SpaceX CEO Elon Musk hopes will carry the first human to Mars one day.

Aired on May 6, 2021

TOEIC-style Questions

1. What did the Starship do for the first time?
   - (A) It landed on the Earth.
   - (B) It launched from Texas.
   - (C) It soared up straight into the sky.
   - (D) It carried humans on board.

2. What is the ultimate goal of the Starship?
   - (A) To land on the Mars
   - (B) To carry vehicles to Mars
   - (C) To be used as a vehicle on Mars
   - (D) To transfer people to Mars from the Earth

Use this page to practice slash listening and shadowing. Circle the subject and underline the verb to understand subject-verb agreement.

ついに着陸成功！
スペースＸの「スターシップ」

For the first time ever, /
SpaceX's Starship Mars prototype has nailed its landing.//
The SN15 rocket launched from south Texas Wednesday, /
soaring straight up 10 kilometers /
before descending safely onto a landing pad.//
It's the fifth spacecraft of its kind /
to attempt such a landing /
but the first to actually stick it.//
Starship is the launch vehicle /
SpaceX CEO Elon Musk hopes /
will carry the first human to Mars one day.//

語注

land successfully: 着陸に成功する	**SN15 rocket:** ▶SN は serial number から	**landing pad:** 着陸場	に炎上するなど、完全な着陸の成功は達成できていなかった
for the first time ever: 史上初めて	**launch:** 〈ロケットなどが〉打ち上げられる	**spacecraft:** 宇宙船	**launch vehicle:** 打ち上げ機、打ち上げ式ロケット
prototype: 試作機、プロトタイプ	**soar:** 飛翔する、空高く舞い上がる	**of its kind:** その種の	
nail: 〜を見事に決める		**attempt:** 〜を試みる	**carry A to B:** A を B へ運ぶ
landing: 着地、着陸	**descend onto:** 〜へと降りる	**stick a landing:** 見事に着陸・着地する ▶これまでは、着陸後	**one day:** いつか、いつの日か

Unit
12

■ ナチュラル音声のアクセント

カナダ英語

■ ニュースのミニ知識

SpaceX（正式名称：Space Exploration Technologies Corp）は、2002年に事業家Elon Musk氏によって設立された宇宙開発企業。2020年には、民間としてはじめて国際宇宙ステーション（ISS）へ宇宙飛行士を運び、その技術力を世界に見せつけた。NASAや米軍と契約し、低コストで物資、機材、宇宙飛行士の輸送を請け負い、宇宙開発ビジネスを成功させている。現在は、会社の最終目標を火星への人類の移住とするが、一般人が、海外旅行を楽しむように宇宙を旅行するには、さらにコストを下げる必要がある。安全で頑強な宇宙船を製造し、何度も繰り返し使える方法での飛行を目指す。今回のロケットの着陸成功は、宇宙船の完全再利用の道筋を示すものとなる。

■ Businessのミニ知識

南アフリカ出身のMusk氏は米国ペンシルベニア大学で物理学とビジネスを専攻、大学院在学中の1995年に起業を果たしている。世界で広く使用されているインターネット決済サービスのPayPalや、電気自動車を販売するTeslaも氏による設立となる。火星を植樹でグリーンにするという目的をもって、ロケット開発会社を設立するなど、奇抜な発想と強い意志で事業を展開している。「インターネット」「クリーンエネルギー」「宇宙」分野で人類の進歩に貢献すると言う。OpenAIやNeuralinkの設立にも関わり、最近では、Twitterを買収している。

Words & Phrases（宇宙開発やロケットに関連した言葉）

□ touchdown	□（飛行機・宇宙船の）着陸、着地
□ satellite	□ 人工衛星
□ terraforming	□ 惑星の地球化、人間が居住可能な環境を作ること
□ space shuttle	□ スペースシャトル、宇宙連絡船
□ space exploration	□ 宇宙探索、宇宙開発
□ space debris	□ スペースデブリ、宇宙ゴミ
□ launch pad	□ ロケットやミサイルの発射台、打ち上げパッド
□ missile launcher	□ ミサイル発射装置
□ intercontinental ballistic missile	□ 大陸間弾道ミサイル：ICBM
□ surface-to-air missile	□ 地対空ミサイル：SAM

■ Let's Think!

宇宙開発ビジネスについて調べ、自分なりの意見や考えを英語で（難しければ日本語で）まとめてみよう。

Unit 13: アマゾンが荷物配達ロボットを試験運用

🔊 Listen and check the words ❶

ナチュラル音声 📻38📻

Listen two times to the news read at natural speed. Check the box for each of the keywords below when you hear them, and look at the definition of each word to understand the news.

definition

☐ invention [ɪnˈvenʃən] : a product or system which has never been created or never existed before

☐ delivery [dɪˈlɪvəri] : the bringing of goods or mail to the place designated, such as to a person's house

☐ accompany [əˈkʌmpəni] : to go together with

☐ nostalgic [nɒˈstældʒɪk] : thinking affectionately about what you experienced in the past

☐ drone [droʊn] : a type of pilotless aircraft directed by remote control

🔊 Listen and check the words ❷

ゆっくり音声［ポーズなし］ 📻40📻

Listen two times to the same news read at slow speed without pauses. Check the box for each of the words or phrases below when you hear them, and write down any other information or expressions you hear.

☐ at first
☐ real-life humans
☐ are weighing in
☐ hops on
☐ what if

Notes

💡 Check your comprehension

What is the news about?

Headline

Choose the best headline for this news.

（A） Real-life Humans Accompany Scouts

（B） Amazon Starts Drone Delivery

（C） Amazon Tests Scout Delivery System

（D） Humans and a Dog Help Scouts' Service

Unit 13

Check the transcript and make sure you understand the content. Then listen to the news again and again until you catch all of it.

Amazon Tests Scout Delivery System

Here it is, the latest George-Jetson-meets-Jeff-Bezos moment: Scout, Amazon's latest invention to make the delivery of packages more efficient and more interesting. It's being tested near Seattle. At first, real-life humans will accompany the six Scouts. Some folks are weighing in, calling them cool and cute; some wondering, "What if a dog hops on and rides?"; others waxing nostalgic for the Amazon drone.

Aired on January 21, 2019

TOEIC-style Questions

1. What did Amazon release?
   (A) A new way of scouting out new talent for executive positions
   (B) A new drone for sending parcels to customers
   (C) A new package delivery system
   (D) Production of a new packaging device

2. What is true about Scout?
   (A) Humans and a dog will help Scout with delivery service.
   (B) George Jetson will develop a futuristic delivery service.
   (C) Scouts have already replaced drones for package delivery.
   (D) Scout will make smooth package delivery possible.

Transcript divided by slashes

ゆっくり音声［ポーズ入り］ 🎧39

Use this page to practice slash listening and shadowing. Circle the subject and underline the verb to understand subject-verb agreement.

アマゾンが荷物配達ロボットを試験運用

Here it is,/

the latest George-Jetson-meets-Jeff-Bezos moment:/

Scout, Amazon's latest invention/

to make the delivery of packages more efficient and more interesting.//

It's being tested near Seattle.//

At first,/

real-life humans will accompany the six Scouts.//

Some folks are weighing in,/

calling them cool and cute;/

some wondering, "What if a dog hops on and rides?";/

others waxing nostalgic for the Amazon drone.//

語注

test:	**invention:**	**weigh in:**	**nostalgic:**
～の試験運転を行う	発明品	意見を加える	郷愁の、追憶の ▶こ
delivery:	**efficient:**	**wonder:**	こでは補語として使わ
配達、配送	効率的な	～だろうかと思う	れている
the latest...:	**real-life:**	**what if:**	**drone:**
最新の…	本物の、実際の	～としたらどうだろう	ドローン
A-meets-B:	**accompany:**	**hop on:**	
AとBを足した	～一緒について行く	飛び乗る	
Jeff Bezos:	**folks:**	**wax:**	
ジェフ・ベゾス ▶米	人々	〈主語の語調が〉～に	
アマゾンCEO		なる	

Unit
13

■ ナチュラル音声のアクセント

イギリス英語

■ ニュースのミニ知識

1文目にthe latest George-Jetson-meets-Jeff-Bezos moment とあるが、George Jetson は、30世紀の宇宙を舞台にしたコメディー・アニメ『The　Jetsons(宇宙家族ジェットソン)』の登場人物。この作品には、自家用ロケットや未来的な家電製品、ロボットなどが登場する。つまりここでのGeorge Jetsonは、空想的かつ未来的な科学技術を象徴するものとして言及されている。

■ Businessのミニ知識

Jeff Bezosは言わずと知れたアマゾンの創業者で、起業家かつe-commerceの先駆者としてこれまでも電子ブックのKindle E-ReaderやAmazon Prime Airというdroneを使った配送システムなど時代の先端を行くサービスを提供してきた。また、Washington Postを買収したり、有人宇宙飛行事業を目的とする民間企業であるBlue Origin(ブルーオリジン 正式名称Blue Origin, LLC)を設立したり、さらには慈善活動にも積極的という多彩な顔を持つ。

Words & Phrases (ネットショッピングに関連した言葉)

□ e-commerce	□ 電子商取引
□ online retailer	□ オンライン小売の 店舗 [販売者]
□ distribution	□ 流通
□ warehouse	□ 倉庫
□ add to cart	□ カートに入れる
□ brick-and-mortar store	□ (オンラインではない) 実際の店
□ artificial intelligence	□ 人工知能
□ autonomous vehicle	□ 自律走行車

■ Let's Think!

Amazonなどのネットショッピングの長所・短所に関して、英語で(難しければ日本語で) まとめてみよう。

Unit 14: ホンダが韓国LGと合弁会社設立へ

🔊 Listen and check the words ❶

ナチュラル音声 41

Listen two times to the news read at natural speed. Check the box for each of the keywords below when you hear them, and look at the definition of each word to understand the news.

definition

- ☐ supply [səplaɪ] : to provide, to make available
- ☐ vehicle [viːɪkᵊl] : something that is used to carry people or goods, such as a car, bus or truck
- ☐ mass [mæs] : a large amount of, a large number of
- ☐ launch [lɔːntʃ] : to make a new product available
- ☐ SUV [es juː viː] : =Sport Utility Vehicle, a type of large car similar to a station wagon
- ☐ decade [dekeɪd] : a period of ten years

🔊 Listen and check the words ❷

ゆっくり音声[ポーズなし] 43

Listen two times to the same news read at slow speed without pauses. Check the box for each of the words or phrases below when you hear them, and write down any other information or expressions you hear.

- ☐ team up
- ☐ mass production
- ☐ prepare for
- ☐ early next year
- ☐ by the end of

Notes

💡 Check your comprehension

What is the news about?

Headline

Choose the best headline for this news.

(A) Honda and LG Energy Solution Team Up

(B) Honda Battles against LG Energy Solution

(C) Honda Solves Energy Problems with EVs

(D) Honda Halts Production of SUVs

Check the transcript and make sure you understand the content. Then listen to the news again and again until you catch all of it.

Honda and LG Energy Solution Team Up

Honda and LG Energy Solution are teaming up to build a nearly $4.5 billion factory in the United States. It will supply LG batteries for Honda's electric vehicles. The companies plan to start building early next year to prepare for mass production by the end of 2025. Honda plans to launch an electric SUV in 2024 and hopes to have 30 EV models by the end of the decade.

Aired on August 30, 2022

TOEIC-style Questions

1. Where is the new factory going to be built?
   (A) In Japan
   (B) In the Republic of Korea
   (C) In the United States of America
   (D) Not decided yet

2. What will they do at the factory?
   (A) Produce batteries
   (B) Construct electric vehicles
   (C) Design electric models
   (D) Build SUV bodies

Use this page to practice slash listening and shadowing. Circle the subject and underline the verb to understand subject-verb agreement.

ホンダが韓国LGと 合弁会社設立へ

Honda and LG Energy Solution are teaming up/
to build a nearly $4.5 billion factory in the United States.//
It will supply LG batteries for Honda's electric vehicles.//
The companies plan to start building early next year/
to prepare for mass production by the end of 2025.//
Honda plans to launch an electric SUV in 2024/
and hopes to have 30 EV models by the end of the
decade.//

語注

LG Energy Solution: ▶韓国財閥LGグループの電池メーカー	**factory:** 工場	**by the end of:** 〜の終わりまでに	**plan to do:** 〜する予定である
team up: 協力する、提携する	**supply:** 〜を供給する	**launch:** （新商品などを）世に出す、売り出す	**decade:** 10年間
nearly: 〜近くの	**electric vehicle:** 電気自動車、EV	**SUV = sport utility vehicle:** スポーツ用多目的車	
4.5 billion: 45億、four and a half billion、なおmillionは100万	**prepare for:** 〜の準備をする **mass production:** 大量生産	**model:** 車種、（機械などの）型、モデル	

Unit 14

■ ナチュラル音声のアクセント

イギリス英語

■ ニュースのミニ知識

創業者である本田宗一郎氏の時代からエンジンへの強いこだわりを持ち、エンジン車によるF1レースでの連続優勝経験も持つHondaが、ついに、エンジン車を全廃して、2040年までに、全世界での販売を電気自動車（EV）と燃料電池車（FCV）にすると発表した。EVの鍵を握るバッテリーは、車用バッテリーで世界トップクラスの位置にある韓国のLG Energy Solution（LGES）と設立する合弁工場から調達するという。HondaとLGESの強力タッグは、内外のEV市場を変える可能性を秘め、国際的にも注目されている。

■ Businessのミニ知識

世界的な気候変動を踏まえて、環境保護の観点から、脱炭素化への取り組みが強化されている。欧米や中国では、ハイブリッド車も含めて、ガソリン車の発売を禁止する動きもある。現在、EVの売り上げ台数では、米国テスラ、中国BYD、上海汽車集団、米国GM、独国フォルクスワーゲンなどが上位を占め、日本車メーカーは出遅れている状態だ。2022年の世界でのEVの売り上げ台数は、すでに自動車販売台数全体の10％に達しているとされ、今後、急速に伸びることが予想される。日本車メーカーは、生き残りをかけて、これまで開発してきたエンジン技術を捨て去るかどうかの決断を迫られている。

Words & Phrases（自動車産業や海外提携に関連した言葉）

□ custom-made product	□ 特注品
□ customization	□ 特注生産
□ mass-customization	□ マス・カスタマイゼーション：部分的に選択を可能にして特注を量産する製造法
□ business alliance	□ 業務提携
□ capital tie-up	□ 資本提携
□ capital and business alliance	□ 資本業務提携
□ joint venture	□ 合弁事業（会社）：JV
□ multinational enterprise	□ 多国籍企業
□ fuel cell vehicle	□ 燃料電池車：FCV
□ decarbonized society	□ 脱炭素化社会

■ Let's Think!

海外企業との提携や海外工場建設について調べ、自分なりの意見や考えを英語で（難しければ日本語で）まとめてみよう。

Unit 15: 労働時間と「幸福度」の関係性 アイスランドの調査で明らかに

🔊 Listen and check the words ❶

ナチュラル音声 44

Listen two times to the news read at natural speed. Check the box for each of the keywords below when you hear them, and look at the definition of each word to understand the news.

definition

☐ trial [traɪəl] : an experiment to test something
☐ weigh [weɪ] : to consider the facts very carefully
☐ postpandemic [poʊstpændemɪk] : after the pandemic
☐ well-being [ˈwɛlˈbiːɪŋ] : the condition of being contented and healthy
☐ productivity [prɒdʊktɪvɪti] : the rate at which goods are produced

🔊 Listen and check the words ❷

ゆっくり音声[ポーズなし] 46

Listen two times to the same news read at slow speed without pauses. Check the box for each of the words or phrases below when you hear them, and write down any other information or expressions you hear.

☐ public-sector employees
☐ took part in
☐ instead of around 40 hours
☐ increased dramatically
☐ stayed the same

Notes

💡 Check your comprehension

What is the news about?

Headline

Choose the best headline for this news.

(A) Less Work Makes Productivity Go Down

(B) How to Do Some Research in Iceland

(C) Trials Show Less Work Is Better

(D) Trials Show More Work Is Better

Unit
15

Check the transcript and make sure you understand the content. Then listen to the news again and again until you catch all of it.

Trials Show Less Work Is Better

As companies weigh a postpandemic future, there are growing conversations about what the workday could look like. Well, Iceland did some research. Public-sector employees took part in two large trials between 2015 and 2019. People worked 35 and 36 hours instead of around 40 hours. The result: worker well-being increased dramatically, and the study found that, even with the shorter hours, productivity either stayed the same or improved.

Aired on July 10, 2021

TOEIC-style Questions

1. What were the results for workers with shorter hours?
   - (A) Satisfaction went down but productivity went up
   - (B) Well-being rose and productivity remained the same or increased
   - (C) Frustration reduced but productivity didn't improve
   - (D) Frustration eased and productivity remained the same or improved

2. Who took part in the two large trials between 2015 and 2019?
   - (A) Companies' employees
   - (B) Companies' employers
   - (C) The politicians in Iceland
   - (D) Public-sector employees

ゆっくり音声［ポーズ入り］ ◖45◗

Use this page to practice slash listening and shadowing.
Circle the subject and underline the verb to understand
subject-verb agreement.

労働時間と「幸福度」の関係性
アイスランドの調査で明らかに

As companies weigh a postpandemic future, /

there are growing conversations /

about what the workday could look like. //

Well, Iceland did some research. //

Public-sector employees took part in two large trials /

between 2015 and 2019. //

People worked 35 and 36 hours / instead of around 40 hours. //

The result: /

worker well-being increased dramatically, /

and the study found that, /

even with the shorter hours, /

productivity either stayed the same or improved. //

語注

trial:	公共部門の、公的機関の	**dramatically:**	**productivity:**
試験、実験	**employee:**	劇的に	生産性
weigh:	従業員、職員	**study:**	**stay the same:**
〜をよく考える、熟考	**take part in:**	研究、調査	同じままである、変わ
する	〜に参加する	**find that:**	らない
postpandemic:	**A instead of B:**	（調べて）〜だと分か	**improve:**
パンデミック後の	BだけではなくA、Bの	る、〜だと結論を出す	向上する
▶ここではポストコロ	代わりにA	**even:**	
ナを指す	**result:**	〜でも、〜にしても	■関連語・派生語
workday:	結果	**hours:**	**be ripe for:**
平日、就業日	**well-being:**	▶ ここ で は working	〜の準備が整った、機
public- sector:	満足度、幸福度	hours（労働時間）のこと	が熟した

Unit
15

■ ナチュラル音声のアクセント

オーストラリア英語

■ ニュースのミニ知識

「ウェルビーイング(well-being)」は、これまで分野に応じて幸福、福利、健康とさまざまに訳されて
きた。総じて、単に身体的な面だけを指すのではなく、精神・社会的な意味を含めて用いられている。
1948年『WHO憲章』(1948)、2017年『ジュネーブ宣言』(2017)においても、「健康(health)」と「ウェ
ルビーイング」が並んで用いられたことからも、それは推察できる。さらに、心理学や企業経営の観
点からも、"well-being"と言う語を用いて、人が満足や幸福を感じるには、どのような環境が必要
であるのかが論じられ、その実現が追求されている。

■ Businessのミニ知識

新型コロナウィルスの影響で、日本においても働き方に変化が起こった。その1つが就労時間の短縮
である。NHKによる2020年「国民生活時間調査」によれば、1日当たりの仕事をした時間の平均は、
男性は7時間51分と1995年の調査から35分減少し、女性は5時間42分と31分減少している。他
には、時差通勤や在宅勤務(リモートワーク)への動きなどの変化がある。一方、在宅勤務では、新
人育成の困難さ、コミュニケーションの取りにくさ等の課題もでている。

Words & Phrases (働き方に関連した言葉)

☐ working hours	☐ 勤務時間
☐ long working hours	☐ 長時間労働
☐ work from home	☐ リモートワーク
☐ off-peak commuting	☐ 時差通勤
☐ flex time system	☐ フレックスタイム制
☐ overtime work	☐ 残業
☐ overtime hours	☐ 残業時間
☐ overtime pay	☐ 残業手当
☐ reduction of overtime work	☐ 残業時間削減
☐ *karoshi*; death from overwork	☐ 過労死

■ Let's Think!

日本における「働きすぎ」の傾向も視野に入れて、人間が健康で幸福に生きるための働き方に関して、
自分なりの意見や考えを英語で(難しければ日本語で)まとめてみよう。

大学生のための
CNN ニュース・リスニング：ビジネス編

2024年1月31日　初版第1刷発行

編著者	JACET関西支部教材開発研究会
	石川 有香
	香林 綾子
	田中 美和子
	松村 優子
	幸重 美津子
発行者	小川 洋一郎
発行所	株式会社 朝日出版社
	〒101-0065 東京都千代田区西神田3-3-5
	TEL：03-3239-0271　FAX：03-3239-0479
	E-MAIL：text-e@asahipress.com
	https://www.asahipress.com/
印刷・製本	錦明印刷株式会社
DTP	有限会社 ファースト
音声編集	ELEC（一般財団法人 英語教育協議会）
装丁	大下 賢一郎